To all those whom I photographed, and who inspired this book.

THE LIVING LEGACY

Produced and published by
Les Éditions Stromboli
C.P. 36586
598, rue Victoria
Saint-Lambert (Québec)
Canada
J4P 3S8
Telephone: 450-465-3657
Fax: 450-465-3749
informations@stromboli.ca
www.stromboli.ca

Publication and artistic coordination: Francesco Bellomo
Text and photographs: Brigitte Bruyez
Adaptation and research: Linda Lapointe
Proof reading, revision: Solange Deschênes
English version: Fred A. Reed
Spanish translation: Analaia Castellari
Graphic design: Langevin et Turcotte
Infography: Joanne Lapointe
Black and white prints, photo digitalization: Le Groupe Corlab
Electronic retouching, production: Francesco Bellomo
Administration, coordination: Gisèle Lambert
Distribution (Canada): Stromboli

Printed in Canada

Dépôt légal 2004
Bibliothèque nationale du Québec
Bibliothèque nationale du Canada
ISBN 2-921800-18-7

Brigitte Bruyez

THE LIVING LEGACY

stromboli

To Ron Feinstein and the team at Lifeline Systems, who believed in this project and made it possible.

CONTENTS

PREFACE

The word Lifeline is used by so many and in so many ways. For me, the word is not just the name of our company, but a term I use to describe what our organization is all about. It is impossible to talk about Lifeline without first noting the solid foundation it is built upon-Passion, Caring and Respect. When you take this base, combine it with the dedicated values and emotions of our almost one thousand employees you create a powerful culture. It is this culture integrated with technology that creates the Lifeline caring service. Over the years, I have been deeply touched by the people we serve. Their thank you notes, kind words and smiles are a constant reminder of how important our work is. A few years back, I asked a distinguished photographer to capture these smiles and thoughts of gratitude in pictures. What I got in return was more than I could have asked for. The exceptionally talented artist Brigitte Bruyez had been able to photograph not just the faces of our subscribers and their caregivers, but the very essence of what it is we do-create peace of mind. I immediately had the extraordinary images enlarged and displayed throughout our offices in the United States and Canada. The impact of these images has been powerfully overwhelming. From employees to visitors to our facilities the feeling has all been the same : pride, satisfaction and joy. These works of art are a true reflection of our culture. It is a beautiful reminder of the difference we make in people's lives. Seeing these faces and knowing that we have been able to improve their quality of life and have them remain in their own homes is invaluable. We have been extremely lucky to find a photographer, an artist, who could so beautifully capture in pictures what it is we do as well as show the wisdom and beauty of aging.

RON FEINSTEIN
Chief Executive Officer
Lifeline Systems

It's about them
It will be you and me
It will be our children
Let's let them know
How much we love them

Brigitte Bruyez 1998

A JOURNEY INTO THE HEART

Early on in my career as a model I was part of a world removed from reality, a world where movement, posture and the human body itself reflected an idealized, overstated definition of beauty derived from images and stereotypes defined by men. When I went on to become a fashion photographer, my work continued to consist of creating dream spaces inhabited by perfect beings and fantasies designed to catch the eye, bound both by the quest for absolute beauty and by the laws of the marketplace. But my esthetic pursuits, based as they were on the obsession with the body and with beauty, could never satisfy me completely. The things that make up a human being—soul, being, strength, weakness—were missing. Missing, above all, was the quality of humanity.

Alongside my work in fashion, I branched out into other areas of art photography, until I began to develop a serious interest in portraiture when for the first time I photographed eldery people on a trip to Mexico in 1985.

But my journey into the universe of the elderly began in 1996, when I made the acquaintance of Ron Feinstein, Chief Executive Officer and President of Lifeline. Ron and I met through his wife Deborah, a museum curator who had consistently supported me and my work. This was at a time when Ron was hoping to commission a series of portraits of his clients, and was looking for someone to bring alive in pictures the humanitarian values of his firm. The images he wanted would be distinguished by love, dignity and respect.

ARLAND
HAROLD AND EVELYNE

Ours was a meeting of the minds: our thinking and our tastes converged as if we had long worked together. I was immediately taken by his project, and by the humanist philosophy that inspired his firm. For him, it was not enough to provide the elderly with a gilded cage of security, but to give them the means to remain active and to contribute, according to their resources, to the growth of society as a whole. As eye-witnesses to the twentieth century, the elderly form a link between the past and the present. Their wisdom and experience are a precious source of wealth for all of us. We must encourage them to speak as often as possible, and listen to them carefully, for they have much to offer us. It is only with this approach in mind that we can build a better society, one in which each of life's ages can find a place.

Early on, Ron warned me that "many of the people you will be photographing today will not see your work in finished form." At first, I was disconcerted; then I came to understand that my work with the elderly could well become precious, perhaps almost sacred, in their eyes, in those of their families, and of all those who loved them. Many of these portraits are the last to be taken. Could there be a greater, more lasting tribute?

Since 1997, Lifeline has introduced me to more than one hundred elderly people of different origins and backgrounds. Each time, on each visit, I was fascinated to discover a unique world. For each of these individuals possessed the wealth of his or her story, of his or her hardships, of his or her joys. Because each life is so distinct, each photo

session had to be adapted to the rhythm and to the life story of each person, to the specifics of each family, to the particularities of each place of residence.

In every case, I did my utmost to establish real relations, and to devote as much time as I could to making emotional contact with my hosts. For me, laughter was the key to creating a relaxed atmosphere and putting them at ease. For this to happen, I could hold nothing back; I had to be with them, entirely at their disposal. They would not have agreed to participate in the adventure if what I asked of them had been sham or superficial. If they gave so completely of themselves, if they agreed to show themselves as they were in front of the camera, it was in response to my deep affection.

Each session was unforgettable, a true gift both for my subjects and for me. It was an occasion for them to put on their best clothes, to speak of those whom they'd loved and lost, to share their memories. They were happy to be alive, to exist, simply to be. I sought out the laughter of years gone by, the joys recalled, and attempted to capture the expressions, the smiles and the looks that revealed them, that made them who they are.

There was to be no retouching, no concealment of wrinkles or physical defects, for there is nothing more beautiful than the truth. The image that resulted is sincere, respectful and revealing.

SARAH

CORA

I also made every effort to convey in my photographs the domestic environment that was familiar to them, that revealed their lives, their concerns, their occupations and their personalities. For me, their everyday objects, their human entourage and the places where they live could teach us as much about them as they themselves. Their memory sings out clearly through beloved objects placed here and there in their living space. I pay close attention to a person's surroundings: family photographs, pets, wedding rings, carefully dusted mementoes, the benevolent presence of a close relative, of a volunteer, to the sound of music close at hand.

All of this passed before my lens; but above all, these photographs reveal, respectfully, sensitively, that which is most precious to the individuals themselves. Here then are the results of my remarkable encounters, presented in a series of unique photographs, a testimony to the many magical moments I am delighted to share now with you.

Each portrait in this series can be seen as an individual image, standing alone and telling a complete story, a life-story, a true story...

MARION AND STEWART

PORTFOLIO

ARLAND AND IRENE

GLADYS

"My granddaughter is my precious gift."

MARION AND STEWART

The dance is silent poetry.
Simonides of Keos (556-467 B.C.)
Greek poet

MARION

One cannot live in the world without playacting now and then.

Chamfort (1741-1794)
French author

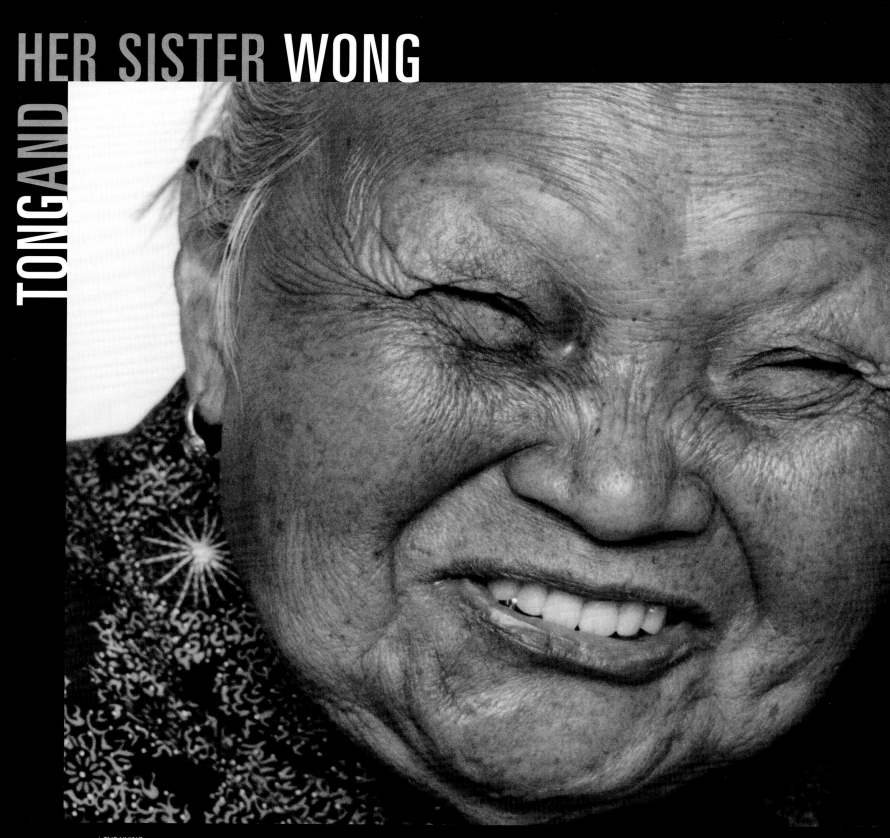

TONGAND HER SISTER WONG

HAROLD
AND
EVELYNE

WALTON

YVETTE

Music lends soul to our hearts and wings to our thoughts.
Plato (428-347 B.C.), Greek philosopher

Music

ELSIE

It takes a long time to become young.
Pablo Picasso (1881-1973)
Spanish painter

VIOLETTE AND FRIEND

"Stay" is a charming word in a friend's vocabulary.

Louisa May Alcott (1832-1888)
American author

ANNE

MARJORIE

Sorrow comes from the solitude of the heart.

Montesquieu (1689-1755)
French author

"As our photo session began,
Marjorie had just lost her life companion.
I could still see the sorrow of absence
in her eyes."

Brigitte Bruyez.

TIM

Life can be long or short; everything depends upon how we live it.

Paulo Coelho (1947-)
Brazilian author

ETHEL WITH HARRY,
A LIFELINE INSTALLER

Nothing is more alive than a memory.

Federico Garcia Lorca (1898-1936)
Spanish poet

Here's what surprises
me about life,
Me, who's in the autumn
of my life,
We forget all our nights
of sadness
But never a morning
of tenderness.

Jean Gabin (1904-1976)
French actor and singer
Extract from *Maintenant je sais*, 1974

NOLAN

BETH

"Today, most people seem obsessed by time. But time is the most precious thing we have."

Beth

HAROLD AND LISBETH

"With my husband, my whole life was truly a honeymoon."

Lisbeth

"During one of my expositions a few years ago, a woman came up to me after having seen my photos of an elderly couple she had known intimately. I related to her how, during the photo session, the wife had told me, with her husband at her side, that her life had been a honeymoon...

The woman broke down and wept, and I realized that they were now dead. She added that they had departed this world one week apart.

I am convinced that their love will unite them for eternity."

Brigitte Bruyez

Truly grown is he who
has not lost his child's heart.
Meng Tsen (372-289 B.C.)
Chinese philosopher.

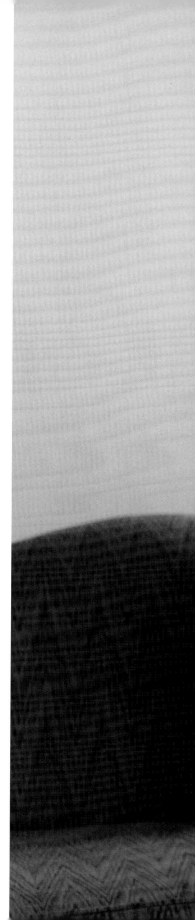

EVELYNE

"It's been a long time since I have laughed... it feels so good!"

Evelyne

FRIENDSHIP

CORA, MARION, MARY-JANE AND MARION

Old age is the best age for friendship.

ELMA
AND HER DAUGHTER THOMASSIMA

"Everybody needs somebody to love
and to be loved."

MILTON

You can see the flame
in young people's eyes
But in an old man's eye,
you see the light.

Victor Hugo (1802-1885)
French author and poet

RUTH

A house needs a grandmother.

Louisa May Alcott (1832-1888)
American author

GENEVIEVE

One tires of everything except learning.
Virgil (70-19 B.C.)
Roman poet

ROSELYNE

Do all things with love.

Og Mandino (1923-1996)

American author

A smile is the kiss of the soul.
Michel Bouthot
Canadian author

THERESA

BRAM
AND HIS SISTER MICKEY

"My brother has a tremendous will to live."

MARIKA

You must be the change you seek in this world.

Gandhi (1869-1948)
Indian philosopher and political figure

MARY

Gentleness is invincible.
Marcus Aurelius (121-180)
Roman Emperor

GERTRUDE

The longer I live the more beautiful life becomes.

Frank Lloyd Wright (1869-1959)
American architect

MARIE

THE LIVING
LEGACY

GLADYS
AND HER DAUGHTER GLORIA

The most serious thing we do on this earth is to love,
the rest hardly matters.

Julien Green (1900-1998)

American-born French author

PAUL

Painting springs from the place where words no longer have meaning.
Gao Xingjian (1940-)
Chinese author

CAROLINE SURROUNDED BY HER GRANDSONS CHRIS AND HENRY

None of us is complete in himself.

Virginia Woolf (1882-1941)
British novelist

SARAH

Sometimes the heart sees what is invisible to the eye.

H. Jackson Brown Jr.
American advertising executive and author

"Enjoy your life and just be thankful you are alive.
From the time you are born, your time is set.
So do what you have to do and be confident."
Sarah

RALPH  AND HIS CAT PUDD

EDITH AND HER FAITHFUL FRANKY

MAURICE

Simplicity is the true form of true greatness.

Francesco de Sanctis (1817-1883)
Italian historian and literary critic

PAULETTE AND GÉRARD

The greatest pleasure in life is to admire the people we love.

Laure Conan (1845-1924)
Canadian author

►8

CÉCILE, HER DAUGHTER SUZANNE AND HER GRANDDAUGHTER CHANTAL

Where can we be happier than among our family?

Jean-François Marmontel (1723-1799)
French author

►9   ►10

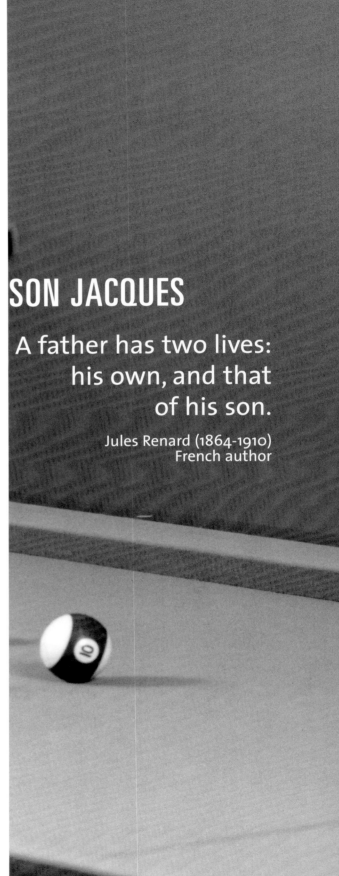

FERNAND AND HIS SON JACQUES

A father has two lives:
his own, and that
of his son.

Jules Renard (1864-1910)
French author

TONY EMBRACED BY GILL AND JUDITH

WALTER AND HIS WIFE JOYCE

When he holds me in his arms,
When he tells me of my charms,
Je vois la vie en rose...

Édith Piaf (1915-1963)
French singer

JOHN
AND HIS BELOVED WIFE VIRGINIA

Life is a work of art that we create at every moment.

Lao Shu (1899-1966)
Chinese novelist and playwright

HOPE ETERNAL

You are not old because you have lived so long. You are not old
because you have wrinkles, less hair, or wear a hearing aid, bifocals,
or walk with an artificial hip.

You are not old until you have lost the desire to absorb the beauty
of nature, to listen for the wonders of music, to feel the change
of seasons, or to meet the challenge of "what's next."

You are only old when you have lost the joy of living.

You are young as long as you have the will, the confidence, and
the courage to do whatever is within your powers to make this earth
a better place for those who follow.

John White

ACKNOWLEDGEMENTS

First and foremost, I would like to thank Ron and Deborah Feinstein for introducing me to a world so different from mine, a discovery that has been a source of deep emotion and endless fascination.

My special thanks to all those who allowed me to enter into their world. Their faces and their stories will remain always engraved on my memory.

I would also like to thank my parents, who communicated to me their love of the arts, and who gave me the precious gift of a good education.

Finally, without the support of my husband Frank, and my daughter Stéphanie, I could never have reached the goals I set for myself. Their love is a daily source of inspiration for me.

My deepest thanks also go to...

All the Lifeline volunteer installers who kept me company over the last few years.

Antonino Treu, and all those who gave me their constant support.

My assistants, and particularly my dear Elva.

Martin Desrochers, Jean Delisle and the entire Groupe Corlab team.

Francesco Bellomo, of Les Éditions Stromboli.

BRIGITTE BRUYEZ

Brigitte Bruyez was born in Le Perreux, France in 1960, into a family of master woodcarvers. Her father, carrying on the family tradition, nurtured Brigitte's artistic talents. When she reached age 12 her parents gave her a camera and introduced her to the elements of design, composition, and to the importance of attention to detail. As she gradually mastered her expressive tools, everyday objects such as flowers and chairs, and even the human body, took on a new dimension. At the same time, alongside the photographer, an athlete, swimmer, dancer and fashion model began to emerge.

Having launched her photographic career in front of the camera, Brigitte Bruyez went on to become a fashion photographer in 1991 while studying at Dawson College in Montreal. After her years as a model, she had made up her mind to step behind the lens, bringing to her new profession her unique experience and knowledge of the human body, its movement and its expressive power. Today she travels frequently for her shoots, but calls three countries home: Canada, Mexico and USA.

Her work has been published in magazines such as Les Ailes de la Mode, Canadian Living, Clin d'oeil, Coup de Pouce, Enfants-Québec, L'Essentiel, Kids Creation, Mariage Québec, Marie-Claire, Photo and Zoom. Advertising campaigns for such companies such as the American Red Cross, Cinar, CN, Forzani, Guess Kids, Krickets, McGill University, Lifeline, Shirmax, Turtle Fur, Orage, and Oshkosh, have played a major role in her development, while her commercial shoots have taken her around the globe. Her career as a fine art photographer has developed rapidly through exhibits in various countries :

ARTIST'S SHOWS

2004   Photographic Display, Lifeline North Arkansas, Arkansas (United States).
        Photographic Display, Lifeline Systems, Toronto, Ontario (Canada).

2003   Photographic Display, Lifeline Systems Inc., Framingham,
        Massachusetts (United States).

2001   Photographic Display, Amers, New York, New York (United States).
        Extremes of Life, Photographic Display, Forum, Montreal, Quebec (Canada).

1999   Photographic Display, Lifeline Systems, Toronto, Ontario (Canada).
        Les fruits de la vie, Photographic Display, Tecton Ind.,
        Longueuil, Quebec (Canada).

1998-2001 Kids, Photographic Display, CN, Les Halles de la Gare,
        Montreal, Quebec (Canada).

1998   Photographic Display, Lifeline Systems, Framingham,
        Massachusetts (United States).
        Photographic Display, Lifeline Systems, Toronto, Ontario (Canada).
        For Art's Sake, Helen Day Art Center, Stowe, , Vermont (United States).

1997   Les fruits de la vie, Galerie de l'Île et Palais de Justice,
        Montreal, Quebec (Canada).
        For Art's Sake, Helen Day Art Center, Stowe, Vermont (United States).

1996   Body and Soul, Helen Day Art Center, Stowe, Vermont (United States).
        Award for excellence.
        La Femme et la Nature, Tecton Industries, Longueuil, Quebec (Canada).
        For Art's Sake, Helen Day Art Center, Stowe, Vermont (United States).
        First prize, photography.

1995   Serenity of Nature, Concours mondial de Photo Magazine, Paris, France.
        Finalist.
        For Art's Sake, Helen Day Art Center, Stowe, Vermont (United States).
        First prize, photography.

1994   For Art's Sake, Helen Day Art Center, Stowe, Vermont (United States).

1993   Los Viejos De Mexico, Gallery Del Arte, Mexico City (Mexico).
        For Art's Sake, Helen Day Art Center, Stowe, Vermont (United States).